Willie Nelson

A Little Golden Book® Biography

T0354055

By Geof Smith

Illustrated by Jeffrey Ebbeler

 A GOLDEN BOOK • NEW YORK

Text copyright © 2023 by Geof Smith
Cover art and interior illustrations copyright © 2023 by Jeffrey Ebbeler
All rights reserved. Published in the United States by Golden Books, an imprint of
Random House Children's Books, a division of Penguin Random House LLC, 1745 Broadway,
New York, NY 10019. Golden Books, A Golden Book, A Little Golden Book, the G colophon,
and the distinctive gold spine are registered trademarks of Penguin Random House LLC.
rhcbooks.com
Educators and librarians, for a variety of teaching tools, visit us at RHTeachersLibrarians.com
Library of Congress Control Number: 2022931983
ISBN 978-0-593-48189-9 (trade) — ISBN 978-0-593-48190-5 (ebook)
Printed in the United States of America
10 9 8 7 6

Willie Hugh Nelson was born on April 29, 1933, in the small town of Abbott, Texas. It was the Great Depression, and times were hard. Though his parents loved their children very much, they thought Willie and his older sister, Bobbie, should live with their grandparents.

Redheaded Willie loved growing up in a small town. He worked on the family farm, played football, and went to the movies almost every Saturday. He especially liked films with singing cowboys, such as Roy Rogers and Gene Autry.

Willie's grandparents encouraged Willie
and Bobbie to play instruments and sing at
church. The first song Willie learned was
"Amazing Grace."

The family radio brought even more music
into their home. Willie enjoyed country and
western singers, but he listened to big bands,
crooners, and jazz, too.

Willie also heard different kinds of music around Abbott. His neighbors from Mexico sang folk songs in Spanish. The townspeople from Czechoslovakia played polkas at their parties. And when Willie worked in the fields, he heard African Americans singing blues songs.

When Willie was five years old, he started making up poems. One year later, his grandfather gave him his first guitar and taught him some chords.

Suddenly, Willie's poems became songs.

Willie played guitar and sang in his first band when he was only ten years old! It wasn't long before he traveled with bands all around Texas, playing in church halls and cowboy hangouts called honky-tonks.

After high school, Willie joined the Air Force, but he had to leave because of problems with his back. Over the next several years, he moved around a lot and tried many jobs.

He was a disc jockey.

He sold vacuum
cleaners door-to-door.

He even repaired saddles.

But Willie never stopped
playing music. Deep down,
he really wanted to be a
country star.

Willie moved to Nashville, Tennessee, in 1960. That was the center of the country music industry. He met many other musicians there and made good friends.

It didn't take long for people to recognize Willie's talent. He wrote songs for other singers to perform. Patsy Cline sang his song "Crazy," and it became one of the most popular songs of all time!

One night in 1969, someone accidentally stepped on Willie's guitar. Willie bought a new one and named it Trigger, after a famous horse from the cowboy movies he'd loved as a child.

Willie has played that guitar ever since. It's now scratched and battered, but it still makes sweet sounds. Friends and other musicians have signed their names on it!

Even with his success, Willie wasn't completely happy in Nashville. The music business there wanted singers to sound and look a certain way. Willie wanted to do his songs in his own style.

Once again, it was time to move on.

In the early 1970s, Willie returned to Texas—
this time to Austin, the state capital. The city was
filled with creative people. The musicians there
mixed rock-and-roll and jazz with country. Willie
really liked the sound!

Willie had begun to let his hair grow. Sometimes he pulled it back into a ponytail or tied it into two braids. He wore old jeans, bandannas, and T-shirts instead of the fancy suits the Nashville stars wore. He wrote songs about the rough-and-tumble lives of cowboys, bandits, and ranch hands.

His music was known as outlaw country, and people loved it.

Eventually, Willie formed a band called the Family. His sister, Bobbie, joined and played piano. They became more popular than he ever could have imagined!

He played shows around the world and sold millions of records. He performed on television, won lots of awards, and also starred in movies.

In 1980, Willie played at the White House for President Jimmy Carter. He even sang a duet with First Lady Rosalynn Carter.

He loved the recognition, but he wanted his fame and songs to help people.

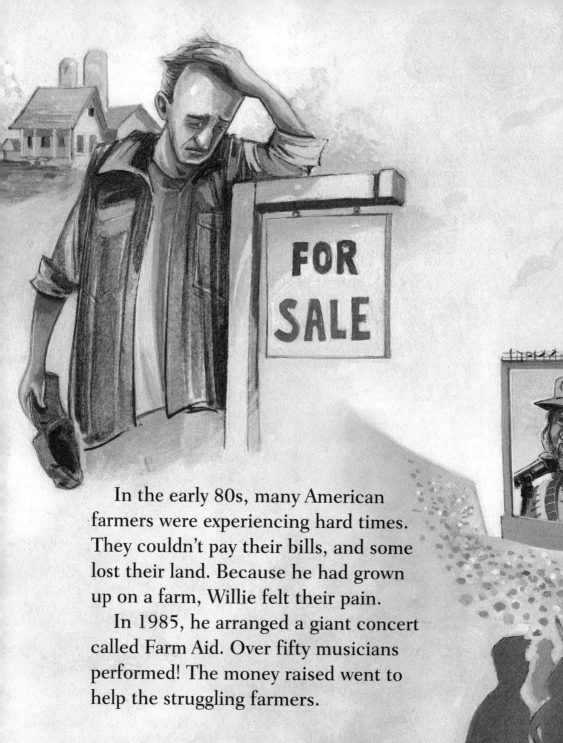

In the early 80s, many American farmers were experiencing hard times. They couldn't pay their bills, and some lost their land. Because he had grown up on a farm, Willie felt their pain.

In 1985, he arranged a giant concert called Farm Aid. Over fifty musicians performed! The money raised went to help the struggling farmers.

But the problem was bigger than Willie had realized. One concert was not enough, so there have been Farm Aid shows almost every year since the very first one.

In later years, Farm Aid also helped people who were affected by natural disasters, like Hurricane Katrina.

When Willie goes to a concert, he likes to travel in his tour bus. That way he can see the countryside. He has had a number of buses over the years, but they've all been called Honeysuckle Rose.

Honeysuckle Rose IV ran on a special
fuel made from corn. It was better for the
environment, and it helped the corn farmers.

Willie bought a large ranch in the hill country outside Austin. His ranch has allowed him to get back to nature. It has also enabled him to help animals. He was especially concerned about horses, so for years he has rescued old, hurt, or mistreated horses and let them run free on his land.

His property is called Luck Ranch. Willie likes
to say, "When you're here, you're in Luck."

Willie has fans around the world, but he's not very different from the little boy who admired the singing cowboys. He still likes to work on his farm and take care of his animals. He enjoys playing songs with his sons and daughters.

And most of all—as he says in his hit song "On the Road Again"—Willie likes traveling from town to town, making music with his friends!